Table

MW01168429

Introduction

Instant Pot is a single piece of equipment that does the work of seven special kitchen tools/appliances and is indeed a multi-cooker that performs the job of an electric pressure cooker, slow cooker, steamer, rice cooker, browning/sauté pan, yogurt maker & warming the pot.

Canadians designed the Instant Pot Electric Pressure Cooker with the objectives of being Secure, Convenient & Dependable. Compared with other electric pressure cookers, you can reduce your electricity usage by up to 70% and it speeds up the cooking time by 2 to 6 times as well.

The best part about Instant Pot is that it preserves all the essential nutrients, vitamins & minerals. It also eliminates the bad microorganisms from food & ensures that the food has the essential minerals & vitamins in it so you can give your loved ones a healthy treat that they deserve. It cooks almost everything. The combination of pressure & steam can make even the toughest food, luscious & tender as a result, Instant Pot helps boosting the digestibility of your food.

Instant Pot is specially designed for you, if you live a fast-paced, green-conscious & health-oriented lifestyle.

Nowadays, the 3rd generation of the pressure cookers presents elegant programming that lets you to modify the temperature, heating intensity, pressure & even the cooking period to your precise needs. Instant pot gives you several options for cooking choice and you can manually control the heat level by the "Adjust" option. You can adjust the cooking time using the + or - feature.

The pressure & temperature inside the Instant Pot is closely monitored by the built-in microprocessor monitors, it also adjusts the duration & heating intensity according to the quantity of food & liquid you have.

The cooking process is entirely automatic, you can factually throw in the ingredients, set it to your preference & walk away. You don't need to watch the timer, adjust the heat, stick by the stove top, or remove the food at the right time to prevent overcooking or undercooking of the food.

You can plan your meal in advance & let it cook later on (for up to 24 hours). It will remind you when the food is cooked. Once you are done with the cooking, it automatically changes to "keep warm" method until you are ready to eat, for up to 10 hours.

It's absolutely quiet, leaves no smell, releases no steam, no spills out, no unnecessary heat in the kitchen so once you are done with the cooking, you would have a clean & pleasant experience with the cooking.

Breakfast Quinoa

Total Preparation & Cooking Time: 25 Minutes
Total Servings: 6

Nutritional Value (Estimated Amount Per Serving)
176 Calories
24 Calories from Fat
2.7g Total Fat
0.0g Trans Fat
0mg Cholesterol
33mg Sodium
256mg Potassium
31.9g Total Carbohydrates
3.1g Dietary Fiber
4.0g Sugars
6.0g Protein

Ingredients:

1 1/2 cups quinoa, uncooked, rinsed well
1/2 Teaspoon vanilla
2 Tablespoons pure maple syrup

1/4 Teaspoon ground cinnamon
2 1/4 cups of water
Pinch of salt

Optional Toppings:
Sliced Almonds
Fresh berries
Milk

Cooking Directions:

Add quinoa together with the maple syrup, cinnamon, water, vanilla & salt into the bottom of your Instant Pot.

Close and lock the lid to its place & cook for a minute, preferably over high pressure. When you are done with the cooking process, turn off the heat; wait 10 minutes and let the pressure release naturally & then release any leftover pressure using the Quick Pressure Release option.

When the valve drops, carefully remove the lid & let allow the steam to disperse.

Fluff well & serve hot with optional toppings of your choice.

Mushroom Risotto

Total Cooking & Preparation Time: 20 Minutes
Servings: About 4

Nutrition Facts (Estimated Amount Per Serving)
291 Calories
48 Calories from Fat
5.3g Total Fat
1.0g Saturated Fat
0.0g Trans Fat
0mg Cholesterol
1178mg Sodium
535mg Potassium
45.0g Total Carbohydrates
3.4g Dietary Fiber
2.2g Sugars
10.3g Protein

Ingredients:

4 Ounces mushrooms, broken or chopped into small pieces
1 Teaspoon of thyme
2 Cups of spinach, fresh

1/2 Cup of white onion minced
1 Cup of Arborio rice
3 Garlic cloves, minced
1/2 cup white wine, dry & at room temperature
1 Tablespoon of vegan butter substitute
3 Cups of vegetable broth, preferably at room temperature
1 ½ Tablespoons of nutritional yeast
1/4 cup of lemon juice, freshly squeezed
1 Tablespoon of olive oil
Black pepper to taste
1 Teaspoon of salt

Cooking Directions:

Preheat your Instant pot using the Sauté option; once hot, add in the oil & sauté the garlic & onions for a couple of minutes

Add in the rice; stir well and then add in the wine, vegetable broth/water, salt, mushrooms & thyme. Close the lid of your Instant pot & turn it to the "sealed" position.

Choose the 'Manual' option; decrease the cooking time to 5 minutes. Once you are done with the cooking, manually release the pressure using the quick release option & carefully remove the lid.

Add in the spinach, nutritional yeast, vegan butter & black pepper; give everything a good stir. Let it sit for some time, preferably at room temperature; if it's still liquid, it would thicken as it cools.

Breakfast Cobbler

Total Preparation & Cooking Time: 25 Minutes
Total Servings: 2

Nutritional Value (Estimated Amount Per Serving)
407 Calories
231 Calories from Fat
25.6g Total Fat
20.7g Saturated Fat
0.0g Trans Fat
0mg Cholesterol
5mg Sodium
320mg Potassium
49.9g Total Carbohydrates
6.8g Dietary Fiber
39.8g Sugars
1.8g Protein

Ingredients:

1 Diced apple
2 Tablespoons sunflower seeds, salted & roasted
1 diced pear

1/4 Cup of pecan pieces
1 Diced plum
2 Tablespoons of maple syrup
1/4 cup of coconut, unsweetened, shredded
3 Tablespoons of coconut oil
1/2 Teaspoons of ground cinnamon
Coconut whipped cream for garnish

Cooking Directions:

1. First place the cut fruit into the bottom of your Instant Pot. Spoon in the coconut oil & maple syrup, sprinkle cinnamon over the top. Close & lock the lid to its place; blocking the pressure valve.

2. Select the Steam option and let cook for 10 minutes. Once you hear the beep coming out of the Instant Pot; release the pressure using the quick-release option.

3. Carefully remove the lid & transfer the cooked fruit into a serving bowl, preferably with a skimmer or slotted spoon. Now place the sunflower seeds, pecans & coconut into the residual liquid; selecting the Sauté option and let everything cook, shifting them on a regular basis and ensure that they don't burn.

4. After 4 to 5 minutes, once they are nicely toasted & browned, remove them & top your cooked fruit.

5. Top with coconut whipped cream & serve warm.

Steel Cut Oats

Total Preparation & Cooking Time: 15 Minutes
Total Servings: 4

Nutritional Value (Estimated Amount Per Serving)
78 Calories
12 Calories from Fat
1.3g Total Fat
0mg Cholesterol
7mg Sodium
76mg Potassium
13.8g Total Carbohydrates
2.1g Dietary Fiber
2.7g Protein

Ingredients:

1 Cup of steel cut oats
Enough water to cover the oats

Cooking Directions:

1. Transfer the steel cut oats into the bottom of your instant pot.

2. Add enough water to cover the oats into the pot.

3. Close & lock the lid to its place, select the manual option; set the cooking time to 3 minutes.

4. Once you hear the beep coming out of the Instant pot, wait for approximately 10 minutes & let the pressure release naturally.

5. Feel free to add toppings of your choice, if desired. Serve & enjoy!

Lentil Risotto

Total Cooking & Preparation Time: 25 Minutes
Servings: About 4

Nutrition Facts (Estimated Amount Per Serving)
387 Calories
4.8g Total Fat
1.1g Saturated Fat
0g Trans Fat
0mg Cholesterol
191mg Sodium
556mg Potassium
70.4g Total Carb
16.7g Dietary Fiber
2.7g Sugars
16g Protein

Ingredients:

1 Cup of Arborio rice
1 Cup of lentils, dry, soaked for overnight
3¼ Cups of vegetable stock

1 Tablespoon of sprigs parsley, leaves & stems chopped
1 Medium chopped onion
2 Cloves garlic mashed lightly
1 stalk celery, chopped
1 Tablespoon of olive oil

Cooking Directions:

Select the sauté option of your Instant Pot and add in the olive oil. Once the oil gets hot; sauté the onion for a minute or two, until just beginning to soften. Now, add in the celery and parsley; sauté for a minute more.

Add in the garlic cloves and rice; mix well & sauté for a minute again, until it's everything in the pot is evenly wet & pearly. Add in the stock & strained lentils; mix well.

Close & lock the lid; select the manual option & set the cooking time to 5 minutes, preferably at high pressure. When the cooking time completes, release the pressure using the Quick Release option and carefully remove the lid. Give everything a good stir & serve immediately with a swirl of extra virgin olive oil.

Lentil Red Curry & Coconut Milk Soup

Total Cooking & Preparation Time: 30 Minutes
Servings: About 4

Nutrition Facts (Estimated Amount Per Serving)
584 Calories
264 Calories from Fat
29.3g Total Fat
23.6g Saturated Fat
0.0g Trans Fat
0mg Cholesterol
799mg Sodium
1371mg Potassium
59.3g Total Carbohydrates
26.4g Dietary Fiber
9.6g Sugars
24.9g Protein

Ingredients:

1 Can of diced tomatoes, don't drain (14 ounce)
1 1/2 Cups of lentils

3 Garlic cloves, minced
1 Onion, large, diced
2 Tablespoons of red curry paste
1/8 Teaspoon of ginger powder
Chopped Spinach to taste
1 Can of coconut milk (15 ounce)
Pinch of red pepper flakes
2 Cups of vegetable broth

Cooking Directions:

Preheat your Instant pot by clicking the "Saute" feature.

Add in the garlic & onion; sauté until starting to brown. Feel free to add a splash of vegetable broth, if it begins to stick.

Once brown, press the "cancel" feature and stop the sautéing process.

Add in the ginger powder, red curry paste & red pepper flakes; give everything a good stir.

Add in the coconut milk, vegetable broth, lentils & diced tomatoes; stir well.

Close & lock the lid; click the "Manual" option & decrease the cooking time to 6 minutes.

Once the cycle completes, wait for some time and let the pressure release naturally. After the valve has completely dropped and all of the pressure is released, carefully remove the lid; stir in the chopped spinach.

Split Pea Soup With Navy Beans & Sweet Potatoes

Total Cooking & Preparation Time: 50 Minutes
Servings: About 6

Nutrition Facts (Estimated Amount Per Serving)
135 Calories
10 Calories from Fat
1.1g Total Fat
0.2g Saturated Fat
0g Trans Fat
0.2mg Cholesterol
410.9mg Sodium
23.1g Total Carbohydrates
9.1g Dietary Fiber
2.5g Sugars
10.5g Protein

Ingredients:

1 Sweet potato, medium, diced
½ Cup of navy beans, dried

18

1 Cup of split peas
¼ - ½ Cup of nutritional yeast to taste
3 Bay of leaves
½ Teaspoon of liquid smoke
5 Cups of water
Pepper & salt to taste

Cooking Directions:

Starting with the water; put everything together (except the nutritional yeast, pepper & salt) to the bottom of your Instant Pot Electric Pressure Cooker.

Close & lock the lid; cook for 20 minutes, preferably on high pressure. Once the cooking time completes, wait for 10 to 15 minutes & let the pressure release naturally.

Carefully remove the lid; stir well & then add in the nutritional yeast, pepper & salt; stir well. Taste & adjust the amount of seasoning, as needed.

Curried Butternut Squash Soup

Total Cooking & Preparation Time: 40 Minutes
Servings: About 6

Nutrition Facts (Estimated Amount Per Serving)
140 Calories
64 Calories from Fat
7.1g Total Fat
4.1g Saturated Fat
0g Trans Fat
0mg Cholesterol
527.7mg Sodium
18.4g Total Carbohydrates
4.3g Dietary Fiber
6.6g Sugars
3.2g Protein

Ingredients:

2 Garlic cloves, minced
1 Onion, large, chopped
1½ Teaspoons of fine sea salt
3 Pounds of butternut squash, peeled & cut into 1" cubes
1 Tablespoon of curry powder

½ Cup of coconut cream or coconut milk
1 Teaspoon of olive oil, extra-virgin
3 cups of water
Optional Toppings:
Dried cranberries
Hulled pumpkin seeds

Cooking Directions:

Select the "sauté" option of your Instant Pot. Once hot, add in the extra virgin olive oil & sauté the onion for 6 to 12 minutes, until tender. Add in the curry powder and garlic; sauté for a minute more, just until fragrant.

For a moment; turn off your Instant Pot and then add in the butternut squash, water & salt into the pot. Close and lock the lid to its position. Choose the "soup" option & let the soup cook for half an hour, preferably at high pressure.

When done, wait for 10 minutes and let the pressure release naturally. After 10 minutes, release any leftover pressure using the Quick Release option.

Carefully remove the lid & puree the soup directly in the pot using an immersion blender.

Stir in the coconut cream or milk & adjust any seasoning to your likings. Top with dried cranberries & hulled pumpkin seeds, if desired. Serve warm.

Mung Bean Stew

Total Cooking & Preparation Time: 40 Minutes
Servings: About 2

Nutrition Facts (Estimated Amount Per Serving)
185 Calories
21 Calories from Fat
2.3g Total Fat
0.4g Saturated Fat
0g Trans Fat
0mg Cholesterol
1195.1mg Sodium
36.2g Total Carbohydrates
7.5g Dietary Fiber
7g Sugars
7.4g Protein

Ingredients:

¼ - ½ Teaspoon cayenne
½ Cup of whole green mung beans, soaked for a minimum period of 15 minutes, dry

1 Teaspoon of ground coriander
½ Cup of brown basmati rice, soaked for 10 minutes
2 Tomatoes, medium, chopped finely
½ Teaspoon cumin seeds
5 Garlic cloves
½ Cup of red onion, chopped
1 Inch of ginger
½ Teaspoon of turmeric
¼ Teaspoon of black pepper
4 Cups of water
½ Teaspoon of garam masala
1 Teaspoon of lemon juice, freshly squeezed
½ Teaspoons of olive oil
Salt to taste

Cooking Directions:

Put onions together with ginger, garlic, tomato, spices & a couple tablespoons of water in a blender; blend on high settings until smooth; set aside.

Click the sauté option of your Instant Pot, preferably on normal heat settings.

When hot, add in the oil & once the oil is hot, then add in the cumin seeds. Roast the seeds until fragrant, for 30 seconds.

Carefully add the puree; stir & cook for 12 to 15 minutes, until smells roasted & the puree thickens. Turn off the sauté option.

Drain the rice & beans and then add them to your Instant Pot. Add lemon juice, water & salt. At this point, add in the chopped veggies; mix well.

Close & lock the lid; select the Manual option and set the cooking time to 10 minutes. Once done, wait for 10 minutes and let the pressure release naturally. After 10 minutes, release any remaining pressure using the Quick Release option.

Taste & adjust the amount of salt & spice. Serve hot with toasted bread or crackers.

Veggie Stew

Total Cooking & Preparation Time: 45 Minutes
Servings: About 8

Nutrition Facts (Estimated Amount Per Serving)
159 Calories
7 Calories from Fat
0.8g Total Fat
0.2g Saturated Fat
0g Trans Fat
0mg Cholesterol
653mg Sodium
32.3g Total Carbohydrates
6.2g Dietary Fiber
8.1g Sugars
5.5g Protein

Ingredients:

For Sauté Mode
8 oz white Mushrooms
1 carrot, minced
½ Teaspoons Rubbed Sage

2 garlic cloves, minced
1 stalk celery, minced
½ onion, minced
1 Teaspoons Rosemary
¼ cup vegetable broth
8 Oz sliced portabella mushrooms, chopped
1 Teaspoons Italian Seasoning
For Manual Mode:
8 oz tomato sauce
½ cup red wine
15 oz tomatoes, diced
1 Tablespoons balsamic vinegar
2 carrots, large, diced
1 Stalk of celery, diced
2 Yukon gold potatoes, diced
½ Teaspoon of kitchen bouquet
3 Cups of vegetable broth
¼ Teaspoon ground pepper
1 Cup of green beans, fresh, diced
½ Teaspoon of salt
To Keep Warm Mode
4 Oz of frozen peas
¾ Cup of pearl onions
2 Tablespoons cornstarch

Cooking Directions:

Select the sauté option of your Instant Pot & sauté the onion, celery, garlic & carrot until soft & translucent, for a couple of minutes.

Add in the Rosemary, Italian Seasoning & sage; stir well & then add in the mushrooms; sauté until all of the liquid is evaporated; don't worry if the veggies stick a little and are slightly brown.

Deglaze the pan using the red wine and then add in the tomatoes, sauce followed by the veggie broth. Add in the leftover veggies (except the peas & pearl onions) & the seasonings. Close and lock the lid to its place and make sure that the release valve is sealing. Select the manual option and set the cooking time to 15 minutes

Once you are done with the cooking, cover with towel & carefully release all of the pressure & steam. Remove the lid; add in the cornstarch, peas & pearl onions. Give everything a good stir & serve warm.

Chickpea & Rice Soup

Total Cooking & Preparation Time: 55 Minutes
Servings: About 6

Nutrition Facts (Estimated Amount Per Serving)
249 Calories
30 Calories from Fat
3.4g Total Fat
0.4g Saturated Fat
0g Trans Fat
0.2mg Cholesterol
794mg Sodium
44.2g Total Carbohydrates
10.5g Dietary Fiber
8.3g Sugars
14.3g Protein

Ingredients:

2 Teaspoons of onion powder
1 Cup of brown rice
2 Teaspoon of garlic powder
1 Cup of chickpeas, dry

8 Cups of water
1 Cup of onion, diced
2 Cups of celery, chopped
½ Cup of nutritional yeast
1 Teaspoon of parsley flakes
2 Cups of carrots, sliced
½ Teaspoon of paprika
2 Teaspoons of salt

Cooking Directions:

Add rice together with chickpeas & half of water to the bottom of your Instant Pot.

Close & lock the lid to its place and make sure that the sealing valve is venting. Select the manual option & set the cooking time to 35 minutes using + or - options.

Once the cooking cycle completes, wait for 10 to 15 minutes and let the pressure release naturally & then carefully remove the lid. Add in the remaining veggies, spices & the leftover water. Give everything a good stir.

Close & lock the lid & vent. Select the manual option again and select the cooking time to 5 minutes. Once you are done with the cooking, let the pressure release naturally.

Vegan Lasagna Soup

Total Cooking & Preparation Time: 04 hours & 15 Minutes
Servings: About 6

Nutrition Facts (Estimated Amount Per Serving)
300 Calories
93 Calories from Fat
10.3g Total Fat
1.6g Saturated Fat
0g Trans Fat
2.3mg Cholesterol
775.3mg Sodium
40.1g Total Carbohydrates
8g Dietary Fiber
5.1g Sugars
14.7g Protein

Ingredients:

For the Pesto Ricotta:
1/4 lb of extra firm tofu, drained

1 Cup of cashews, raw, soaked in water for 4 to 8 hours, drained & rinsed
1/4 cup almond or soy milk, unflavored
3 to 4 Tablespoons of prepared vegan pesto or to taste
1 Tablespoon of lemon juice, freshly squeezed
Pepper & salt to taste

For the Lasagna Soup:
1 Can of tomatoes, diced (14 ounce)
8 Lasagna noodles, broken into pieces
1 Teaspoon of basil, dried
4 1/2 Cups of vegetable broth
1 Onion, medium, diced
3 Cloves of garlic, minced
1 Can of tomatoes, crushed (14 ounce)
3/4 Cup of brown lentils, dried
1 Teaspoon of dried oregano
3 Cups of spinach leaves, fresh & chopped

Cooking Directions:

First put the onion together with broth, basil, garlic, lentils & oregano into the bottom of your Instant Pot; stir couple of times to blend. Select the slow cooker setting of your Instant & cover. Cook for 2 hours, preferably on high settings, until the lentils are just firm.

Add in the crushed & diced tomatoes to the Instant pot; stir well & continue cooking for 2 to 3 more hours, preferably on high.

Add spinach and noodles; give everything a good stir & cook for 10 to 12 minutes, until spinach is wilted & the noodles are tender.

Season with pepper & salt to taste.

Now, place the soaked cashews & milk into a food processor & blend on high settings until smooth. Add in the tofu; a pulse couple of times, until the mixture just takes on a ricotta-like texture. Add lemon juice, pesto & season with pepper and salt to taste.

Divide the soup evenly into the bowls & top each bowl with a dollop of vegan pesto ricotta. Serve & enjoy!

White Bean Stew with Kale & Winter Squash

Total Cooking & Preparation Time: 01 hour & 20 Minutes
Servings: About 6

Nutrition Facts (Estimated Amount Per Serving)
205 Calories
15 Calories from Fat
1.7g Total Fat
0.3g Saturated Fat
0g Trans Fat
0mg Cholesterol
443.9mg Sodium
42.3g Total Carbohydrates
14.1g Dietary Fiber
8g Sugars
9.8g Protein

Ingredients:

1 Teaspoons. basil, dried

1 pound winter squash, cubed or peeled pumpkin, cut into ¾"
dice
4 Teaspoons. smoked paprika, divided
1 lb. navy beans, dried, quick soaked or soaked for overnight
4 garlic cloves, minced
1 cup corn, fresh or frozen
2 Teaspoons of oregano, dried, divided
1 onion, large, chopped
1 1/2 Teaspoons of cumin, ground, divided
1 Red bell of pepper, large, chopped
1 Jalapeño pepper, seeded & chopped finely
1 Can of tomatoes, diced, fire-roasted (15 ounce)
1/2 Cup of basil, fresh, chopped
1 Bunch of kale, stems removed & sliced
5 cups water
1 Teaspoon of salt to taste

Cooking Directions:

Select the sauté option of your Instant pot and then add in the
onions & a pinch of baking soda. Cook for a couple of
minutes, until onion begins to brown & is soft. Add in the garlic
& cook for a minute more.

Add in the beans, 1 Teaspoon of oregano, 2 Teaspoons of
paprika, dried basil, 1 Teaspoon of cumin & water, to the pot.
Close and lock the lid to its place; select the manual option
and set the cooking time to 8 minutes, preferably at high
pressure & then using the quick release option, release all of
the pressure.

Carefully remove the lid and then add in the squash along with
the tomatoes, leftover peppers, seasonings & salt. Close and
lock the lid again & cook for 8 more minutes, preferably at high
pressure. Once the cooking cycle completes, wait for 10
minutes and let the pressure release naturally; and then
perform a quick release.

Check & taste the amount of seasoning; add more of oregano, cumin, or salt to taste. Add in the corn and kale; let simmer until the kale is tender, preferably covered. Add in the basil; stir well & cook for a minute again, before serving.

Peanut & Sweet Potato Stew

Total Cooking & Preparation Time: 55 Minutes
Servings: About 4

Nutrition Facts (Estimated Amount Per Serving)
457 Calories
220 Calories from Fat
24.4g Total Fat
4.3g Saturated Fat
0g Trans Fat
0mg Cholesterol
683mg Sodium
47.8g Total Carbohydrates
15.9g Dietary Fiber
12g Sugars
18.8g Protein

Ingredients:

2 Cups of hearty leafy greens such as kale, arugula, spinach, collard
1 Tablespoon of ginger, fresh, minced
3 Garlic of cloves, finely minced
1 Onion, medium, minced finely
½ Teaspoon of red chili pepper, crushed

1 Sweet potato, medium, peeled & diced
½ Cup of almond or peanut or sunflower butter
1 Teaspoon of coriander, dried
2 Cups of vegetable broth
1 Can of diced or crushed tomatoes (14.5 Oz)
1 ½ Cups of peas, frozen or corn, canned/frozen
1 Can of black or kidney beans, drained & rinsed
2 Tablespoons of olive oil
Salt & pepper to taste

Cooking Directions:

Blend the can of diced tomatoes along with their accumulated juice, if using for a couple of seconds in a blender or food processor.

Press the sauté option of your instant pot and sauté the onion for a couple of minutes, until soft but not brown.

Add in the ginger, garlic & chili; cook for a couple of minutes until soften.

Add in the tomatoes; stir several times until well combined, then add in the peanut/almond butter & coriander, stirring frequently until smooth.

Add in the sweet potatoes & broth; stir well. Close and lock the lid and cook on manual settings for 10 minutes, until the sweet potatoes are tender.

Add the peas/corn, black beans and greens; cook until the greens are wilted & the peas/corn & beans are heated through.

Season with pepper and salt to taste and then add in more of crushed chili flakes to your likings.

Refried Beans

Total Cooking & Preparation Time: 50 Minutes
Servings: About 4

Nutrition Facts (Estimated Amount Per Serving)
369 Calories
14 Calories from Fat
1.6g Total Fat
0mg Cholesterol
803mg Sodium
1547mg Potassium
67.9g Total Carbohydrates
16.9g Dietary Fiber
4.8g Sugars
22.1g Protein

Ingredients:

1 onion, large, cut into fourths
2 cups pinto beans, rinsed well, dried (don't soak)
1 Teaspoon of cumin
4 Garlic cloves, peeled & chopped roughly
1 Jalapeno, seeded or to taste
1/2 Teaspoon of black pepper

1 Teaspoon of paprika
1/2 Cup of salsa
1 Teaspoon of chili powder
3 Cups of water or vegetable broth or both
Cilantro, fresh to taste
1 Teaspoon of salt

Cooking Directions:

Add everything to the bottom of your instant pot; stir well.

Close & lock the lid; turning the steam valve to the "sealed" position.

Choose the "Manual" option & decrease the cooking time to 28 minutes.

When the cooking cycle completes, wait for a minimum period of 10 minutes and let the pressure release naturally and then carefully remove the pressure using the quick release option. Carefully remove the lid, give everything a good stir.

Using a high speed blender; carefully blend the beans until you get your desired consistency (as it would be very hot). Serve warm.

Delicious Pasta

Total Cooking & Preparation Time: 30 Minutes
Servings: About 8

Nutrition Facts (Estimated Amount Per Serving)
262 Calories
6.2g Total Fat
1g Saturated Fat
0g Trans Fat
41mg Cholesterol
499mg Sodium
218mg Potassium
42.1g Total Carb
3.3g Dietary Fiber
5.4g Sugars
9g Protein

Ingredients:

1 Bag of organic Broccoli, frozen (10 ounce)
1 Box of Organic Pasta (16 ounce)
4 Quarts water
1 Jar of Organic Tomato Basil Pasta Sauce (25 ounce)

Cooking Directions:

Bring water to a boil & then dump in the pasta; stir quickly.

Ensure that you set the cooking time 5 minutes less than the cooking time mentioned on the box.

When the cooking cycle completes, add in the broccoli florets; press the manual option again and set the cooking time to pending time which was left earlier.

When the timer goes off, drain the broccoli and pasta; transfer both into the sauce. Stir & heat until the sauce has warmed up, preferably on low heat settings.

Tempting Tofu

Total Cooking & Preparation Time: 25 Minutes
Servings: About 4

Nutrition Facts (Estimated Amount Per Serving)
247 Calories
35 Calories from Fat
3.9g Total Fat
0.8g Saturated Fat
0g Trans Fat
0.1mg Cholesterol
996.1mg Sodium
44.4g Total Carbohydrates
5.6g Dietary Fiber
14.5g Sugars
10.5g Protein

Ingredients:

For Instant Pot Ingredients:
1 cup carrot coins
1 heaping tsp. organic corn starch
¼ cup onions, sliced

1 package firm or extra firm tofu, cut into cubes (14 ounces)

For Sauce Ingredients:
½ cup water
¼ cup gluten free soy sauce
3 tbsp. nutritional yeast
3 tbsp. agave nectar or maple syrup
1 tbsp. minced ginger
½ tbsp. rice vinegar
1 tsp. garlic, minced

For Serving:
Cooked quinoa, brown rice or other grain
Lettuce leaves, fresh to make wraps

Cooking Directions:

Mix all of the sauce ingredients together in a large bowl; set aside.

Layer the carrots & onion on the bottom of your Instant pot and then place the tofu over the top. Evenly transfer the sauce over the tofu. Select the slow cooker option of your Instant pot & cook for 7 to 9 hours, preferably on low heat settings.

If you want your sauce to be a little thicker then mix the cornstarch with approximately 1 or 2 tbsp. of water; mix well until completely dissolved and then add the mixture to the instant pot; mix well. Turn to high heat settings & cook for 15 minutes more.

Serve in lettuce to make lettuce wraps or over your favorite cooked grain.

Delicious Pie

Total Cooking & Preparation Time: 25 Minutes
Servings: About 4

Nutrition Facts (Estimated Amount Per Serving)
163 Calories
7 Calories from Fat
0.7g Total Fat
0.2g Saturated Fat
0g Trans Fat
0mg Cholesterol
725.7mg Sodium
33.4g Total Carbohydrates
8g Dietary Fiber
9.8g Sugars
7.5g Protein

Ingredients:

1 Cup of tomatoes, fresh, diced or canned
1/2 Cup of carrot, diced
1 Cup of onion, diced
1/2 Cup of sweet potato, peeled or turnip, diced
1 Cup of French green lentils, rinsed & picked over

1/3 Cup of celery, diced
1 Teaspoon of thyme, dried
1¾ cups of vegetable stock
1 Bay leaf
1/2 Teaspoon of rosemary, fresh & chopped or ¼ Teaspoon dried
1 Garlic of Parsley Mashed Potatoes recipe
1 to 2 Tablespoons of browned rice flour
1 Tablespoon of tomato paste
1 to 2 Teaspoons of tamari, to taste
1 Tablespoon of vegan Worcestershire sauce

Cooking Directions:

Preheat your Instant pot by pressing the sauté option. Add in the onion, celery, and carrot; dry sauté a couple of minutes. Add in the lentils, turnip, bay leaf, thyme, stock & rosemary.

Close and lock the lid to its place. Select the manual option and set the cooking time to 10 minutes, preferably at high pressure. Once you are done with the cooking, wait for 10 minutes and let the pressure release naturally. Once all the pressure is removed, carefully remove the lid.

Add a Tablespoon of the browned flour, followed by the tamari, Worcestershire sauce, tomato paste & tomatoes; give everything a good stir. Lock the lid again & let sit for a couple of more minutes and then release any built-up pressure using the quick release option.

Transfer the filling to a large casserole dish; discarding the bay leaf. Top the cooked pie with the mashed potatoes. Heat the potatoes or run them under the broiler until brown.

Delicious Dumplings

Total Cooking & Preparation Time: 35 Minutes
Servings: About 4

Nutrition Facts (Estimated Amount Per Serving)
299 Calories
91 Calories from Fat
10.1g Total Fat
1.8g Saturated Fat
0g Trans Fat
3.4mg Cholesterol
1268.9mg Sodium
44.9g Total Carbohydrates
3.8g Dietary Fiber
4.8g Sugars
8.4g Protein

Ingredients:

1 Teaspoon of ginger, fresh, grated
½ Cup of carrot, shredded
1 Cup of white mushrooms or shiitake mushrooms, minced
1½ Cups of cabbage, minced
1 Tablespoon of oil

2 Tablespoons of soy sauce
1 Tablespoon of rice wine vinegar
12 Rounds dumpling wrappers
1 Teaspoon of sesame oil

Cooking Directions:

Over medium heat in a large pan; heat the oil & add in the minced mushrooms. Sauté for a couple of minutes, until you see the juices coming out of the mushrooms and then add in the carrot, cabbage, vinegar & soy sauce; sauté until mixture becomes dry.

Get rid of the liner from your Instant Pot & set on a pot holder or on the stove; add in the sesame oil & ginger; mix well.

Lightly coat a vegetable steamer with oil and then place it in your Instant Pot. Set a small size bowl filled with water subsequently to the cutting board. On the cutting board, arrange a wrapper & using your fingertip; spread the water just about the edge. Add a Tablespoon of the filling to the center & fold the wrapper in half, don't forget to match the edges. Press the edges together.

Add 1 and ½ cups of water & the rack to the Instant Pot and then place the steamer lower into the pot. Place the lid on your Instant pot & ensure that the handle of the steam release is sealed. Choose setting & decrease the cooking time to 6 minutes. Once done with the cooking; manually release the pressure using the Quick Release option.

Cauliflower Rice

Total Cooking & Preparation Time: 25 Minutes
Servings: About 4

Nutrition Facts (Estimated Amount Per Serving)
100 Calories
67 Calories from Fat
7.5g Total Fat
1g Saturated Fat
0g Trans Fat
0mg Cholesterol
168.5mg Sodium
8g Total Carbohydrates
3.9g Dietary Fiber
3.3g Sugars
2.9g Protein

Ingredients:

½ Teaspoon of parsley, dried
1 Head of cauliflower, medium to large, washed & trim the leaves off & chopped
¼ Teaspoon of salt or to taste

2 Tablespoons of olive oil

Optional Seasonings:
¼ Teaspoons of cumin
Cilantro, fresh
¼ Teaspoon of turmeric
Lime juice or lime wedges, fresh
¼ Teaspoon of paprika

Cooking Directions:

Put the cauliflower pieces into the steamer and then insert it into your Instant Pot. Add a cup of water in the steamer basket. Close & lock the lid to its place; ensure that the valve is sealed. Press the manual settings and cook for a minute, preferably at high pressure.

Once the cooking cycle completes, use the quick-release option and then carefully remove the lid. Transfer the cooked cauliflower pieces to a large plate. Transfer the water in the pot & return the pot to the Instant pot; press the cancel option and then select the sauté option. Add oil to the bottom of the pot & then add in the cooked cauliflower, using a potato mashed, break up the pieces.

Add in your desired spices while heating & stirring. For a delicious "lime cilantro" version, squeeze the lime juice & sprinkle the fresh cilantro. Serve warm & enjoy.

Mouthwatering Marinara Sauce

Total Cooking & Preparation Time: 25 Minutes
Servings: About 4

Nutrition Facts (Estimated Amount Per Serving)
94 Calories
2 Calories from Fat
0.2g Total Fat
0g Saturated Fat
0g Trans Fat
0mg Cholesterol
666.3mg Sodium
20.1g Total Carbohydrates
4.1g Dietary Fiber
5.2g Sugars
3.5g Protein

Ingredients:

2 Sweet potato, large, diced (approximately 1 cup)
1 1/2 Cups of water
2 Cans of crushed tomatoes (28 Oz)
1/2 Cup of red lentils, remove any shriveled lentils or stones, then rinse in a fine mesh sieve

2 to 3 Garlic of minced cloves,
1 Teaspoon of salt or to taste

Cooking Directions:

Select the sauté option of your Instant pot and then sauté the lentils, garlic, sweet potatoes & salt for a minute or two, until the garlic starts to bring out the flavor.

Add in the crushed tomatoes & water; stir well and ensure that the lentils don't stick to the bottom.

Bring it to high pressure & cook for 12 minutes.

Once you are done with the cooking process, wait for 10 minutes and let the pressure release naturally. Once all of the pressure is removed, carefully remove the lid

Give everything a good stir until just combined & puree with an immersion blender, if desired.

Garlic Mashed Potatoes

Total Cooking & Preparation Time: 25 Minutes
Servings: About 4

Nutrition Facts (Estimated Amount Per Serving)
146 Calories
6 Calories from Fat
0.6g Total Fat
0mg Cholesterol
250mg Sodium
815mg Potassium
32.4g Total Carbohydrates
2.5g Dietary Fiber
1.4g Sugars
5.1g Protein

Ingredients:

1 Cup of vegetable broth
4 Russet, Yukon or yellow fin gold potatoes, medium (cut each potato into 8 to12 chunks)
1/2 Cup of non-dairy milk

6 Garlic of cloves, peeled & cut in half
1/4 Cup of parsley, fresh, chopped
Salt

Cooking Directions:

Put the potato pieces with the garlic & the broth into the bottom of your Instant pot electric pressure cooker.

Close & lock the lid; turning the steam valve to "sealed" position.

Press the "Manual" option & decrease the cooking time to 4 minutes.

When the cooking cycle completes, move the pressure valve to "venting" & let the pressure release. Carefully remove the lid as everything would be too hot.

Using a hand blender or a masher; mash the potatoes until you get your desired consistency and then add all of the soy milk.

Add parsley and salt to taste; stir well until everything is well combined.

Serve hot.

Coconut Quinoa Curry

Total Cooking & Preparation Time: 04 hours & 25 Minutes
Servings: About 6

Nutrition Facts (Estimated Amount Per Serving)
412 Calories
93 Calories from Fat
10.3g Total Fat
7.5g Saturated Fat
0g Trans Fat
0.1mg Cholesterol
492.7mg Sodium
72.1g Total Carbohydrates
13.7g Dietary Fiber
14.4g Sugars
13.7g Protein

Ingredients:

1 Tablespoon of garlic cloves, minced
2 Cans of coconut milk (14.5 ounce each)
1 Can of diced tomatoes (28 ounce)
2 Cups of broccoli crowns, large, cut into florets

1 Cup of white onion, diced
3 Cups of sweet potato, peeled, chopped
1 Can of organic chickpeas, drained & rinsed (15 ounce)
¼ Cup of quinoa
1 Tablespoon of turmeric, freshly grated
2 Teaspoons of tamari sauce, wheat free
1 Tablespoons of ginger, freshly grated
½ - 1 Teaspoon of chili flakes
1 Teaspoon of tamari or miso

Cooking Directions:

Starting with 1 cup of water; put everything together to the bottom of your Instant pot. Stir well until everything is completely incorporated.

Close and lock the lid & cook until the curry has thickened & sweet potato is cooked through, for 3 to 4 hours, preferably on high heat settings

Instant Pot Lentil Bolognese

Total Cooking & Preparation Time: 45 Minutes
Servings: About 4

Nutrition Facts (Estimated Amount Per Serving)
137 Calories
10 Calories from Fat
1.1g Total Fat
0.2g Saturated Fat
0g Trans Fat
0mg Cholesterol
763.7mg Sodium
28g Total Carbohydrates
9g Dietary Fiber
9.9g Sugars
7.6g Protein

Ingredients:

3 Carrots, medium, diced
1 Cup of Beluga black lentils, washed
4 Garlic of cloves, minced
1 Can of fire roasted tomatoes, chopped (28 ounce)
Red pepper flakes to taste
2 Tablespoons of Italian seasonings, dry

1 Can of tomato paste
Pepper & salt to taste
4 Cups of water
Balsamic vinegar to taste
1 Yellow onion, diced

Cooking Directions:

Put everything together (except the pepper, salt & vinegar) into the bottom of your Instant Pot; stir well until all the ingredients are well incorporated. Close & lock the lid; click the manual option and set the cooking time cook to 15 minutes.

When you are done with the cooking, wait for 10 to 15 minutes and let the pressure release naturally.

Once all of the pressure is released, carefully remove the lid and add a drizzle of balsamic; stir well.

Taste & adjust the amount of seasonings and balsamic vinegar to your likings. Serve over your desired pasta.

Spinach Chana Masala

Total Cooking & Preparation Time: 40 Minutes
Servings: About 6

Nutrition Facts (Estimated Amount Per Serving)
362 Calories
134 Calories from Fat
14.9g Total Fat
1.4g Saturated Fat
0.1g Trans Fat
0mg Cholesterol
635.5mg Sodium
46.4g Total Carbohydrates
10.4g Dietary Fiber
9.8g Sugars
14.3g Protein

Ingredients:

1 cup chana/ cholay/chickpeas, raw, soaked for overnight
1 cup onions, chopped
3 tbsp. cooking oil
1 bay leaf

½ tbsp. ginger, grated
2 cups tomato puree, fresh
1 tbsp. garlic, grated
1.5 cups water
1 tbsp. chickpea flour, roasted
Spices needed
1 tbsp. chana masala/cholay
½ tsp. turmeric
1 green chili, chopped finely
2 tsp. chili powder
1 tsp. coriander powder
To be added later
2 cups baby spinach, fresh, chopped
Lemon, fresh
Fistful of cilantro, fresh, chopped
Salt to taste

Cooking Directions:

In a clean mesh; wash the chickpeas under cold & running water for half a minute.

The next morning; drain out all the excess water from the soaked chickpeas. Turn on your Instant pot and click the sauté option. After couple of minutes; add in 3 tbsp. of the cooking oil & sauté the onions until translucent, for a minute or two.

Add in the green chili, bay leaf, ginger & garlic paste; cook for half a minute. Add in the chili powder, turmeric, chana masala and coriander powder along with 1 tbsp. of water (to prevent the masala to burn).

Sauté for couple of more seconds; stir well. Add in the roasted chickpea flour and sauté for some more seconds. Now add in the drained chickpeas, tomato puree & 1.5 cups of water; mix well.

Close & lock the lid, position the steam release to sealing position; select the manual option and set the cooking time to 15 minutes, preferably on High pressure.

Once the cooking time completes, wait for 10 to 15 minutes and let the pressure to release naturally. After 15 minutes, remove any excess pressure using the Quick Release option and carefully remove the lid; stir well & smash a chickpea to check the doneness.

Now select the instant pot on to the sauté mode again & add in the chopped spinach & salt. For thicker gravy, using the back of a spoon; mash few chickpeas.

Let cook on to the sauté mode for couple of minutes and turn off your instant pot. Add in some lemon juice & chopped coriander. Taste & adjust the amount of spices & serve warm as a soup, along with chapatti or over quinoa/rice

Lentil & Spinach Dal

Total Cooking & Preparation Time: 30 Minutes
Servings: About 6

Nutrition Facts (Estimated Amount Per Serving)
210Calories
2.7g Total Fat
1.4g Saturated Fat
0g Trans Fat
3mg Cholesterol
233mg Sodium
734mg Potassium
35.2g Total Carb
14.2g Dietary Fiber
6g Sugars
13.5g Protein

Ingredients:

1 Red or yellow onion, large, chopped
3 Garlic cloves, minced
1 Teaspoon of ground coriander
4 Cups of spinach, fresh
1 Teaspoon of ground turmeric

1 ½ Cups of yellow split peas or red lentils or combination of both
3 Cups of water
1 Tomato, large, cut into 6 to 8 wedges
2 Teaspoons of vegan butter
1 Teaspoon of ground cumin
1/4 Cup of cilantro, fresh, chopped
2 Tablespoons of olive or coconut oil
1/4 Teaspoon of cayenne pepper, dried
1/2 Teaspoons salt
To serve:
Fresh cilantro
Plain yogurt
Cooked naan or brown rice

Cooking Directions:

Press the sauté option of your Instant pot and then heat the olive or coconut oil. Once hot, add in the chopped onions; cook for a couple of minutes, until soft & translucent. Add in the garlic, stir well & cook until fragrant, for a minute more. Press the cancel option & turn off the heat, then add in the coriander, cumin, cayenne & turmeric; mix until combined well.

Add in the lentils, tomato wedges, water and salt into the onion mixture; stir well. Close and lock the lid; ensure that the valve is in the sealed position.

Hit the 'Manual' option and set the cooking time to 10 minutes. Once the cooking cycle completes, select the 'Cancel' option and turn off the warming mode. Wait for 10 to 15 minutes and let the pressure release naturally, after 10 minutes release any leftover pressure using the quick release option.

Remove & discard the tomato skins; whisk together the lentils to blend; if required, feel free to smash the tomato wedges against the side of the pot. Add in the spinach together with the cilantro and vegan butter; stir several times to combine.

Top it with plain yogurt & fresh cilantro and serve with naan or over brown rice.

Sassy Sesame Tofu

Total Cooking & Preparation Time: 30 Minutes
Servings: About 4

Nutrition Facts (Estimated Amount Per Serving)
283 Calories
13.6g Total Fat
2.2g Saturated Fat
0g Trans Fat
0mg Cholesterol
360mg Sodium
765mg Potassium
27.3g Total Carb
7.3g Dietary Fiber
9.3g Sugars
16.1g Protein

Ingredients:

2 Teaspoons of sesame oil, toasted
1 Cup of sweet potato, peeled, diced
2 Tablespoons. sesame seeds
1 carrot, peeled & cut diagonally into ½" pieces
3 Garlic cloves, minced

1/3 Cup of vegetable stock
2 Cups of snow peas or sugar snap, cut in half
1 Pound of extra firm tofu, cut into 1" cubes
2 Tablespoons of sweet & spicy red pepper sauce or sriracha
1 to 2 Tablespoons of tamari
2 Tablespoons of scallion, chopped
1 Tablespoon of rice vinegar
2 cups white, yellow, or sweet onion, medium, sliced from top to bottom
2 Tablespoons. tahini

Cooking Directions:

Select the sauté option of your Instant pot and add in the sesame oil. Once hot, add in the onion, sweet potato, and carrot; sauté for a minute or two. Add in the garlic & 1 Tablespoon of sesame seeds; sauté for a minute more. Add in the tofu, vinegar, tamari & stock.

Close and lock the lid to its place; bringing to high pressure & cook for 2 to 3 minutes. Release the pressure manually using the Quick Release option. Carefully remove the lid and add the peas; lock the lid again & cook for a minute, preferably on low heat settings. Release the pressure again using the Quick Release option. Carefully remove the lid & stir in the tahini and pepper sauce.

Garnish with the leftover 1 Tablespoon of sesame seeds & the green onions, chopped. Serve & enjoy.

Tomato Stewed Green Bean

Total Cooking & Preparation Time: 25 Minutes
Servings: About 4

Nutrition Facts (Estimated Amount Per Serving)
95 Calories
45 Calories from Fat
5g Total Fat
0.7g Saturated Fat
0g Trans Fat
0mg Cholesterol
70.4mg Sodium
12.4g Total Carbohydrates
4.6g Dietary Fiber
6.3g Sugars
2.9g Protein

Ingredients:

1 Pound of green beans (frozen or fresh), remove the ends
1 Clove of garlic, crushed
1 Sprig basil, leaves removed
2 Cups of fresh, chopped tomatoes
1 Tablespoon of olive oil
1 Teaspoon of extra virgin olive oil

2 Pinches of salt

Cooking Directions:

Preheat your Instant pot by pressing the sauté option. Once hot, add a swirl of olive oil & then add in the crushed garlic clove, preferably without the lid and over medium heat settings.

When the garlic turns golden, add in the tomatoes; swirl everything around. Now, add in the steamer basket and fill it with the green beans.

Sprinkle salt over the beans. Close & lock the lid to its place; press the manual option & set the cooking time to 5 minutes, preferably on high pressure.

When the cooking time completes, release the pressure using the quick release option and carefully remove the lid. Remove the steamer basket & insert the trivet; tumble the green beans out of it into the base of your Instant cooker; mix the green beans with the tomato sauce.

Check for doneness & cook them together with the sauce on low heat settings in the Instant Pot cooker, if the green beans need to cook a little more, preferably without the lid. Move the green beans to a large serving bowl, when fork tender. Sprinkle with fresh basil leaves & a swirl of olive oil. Serve warm or let cool a bit at room temperature.

Coconut Tofu Curry

Total Cooking & Preparation Time: 25 Minutes
Servings: About 4

Nutrition Facts (Estimated Amount Per Serving)
259 Calories
124 Calories from Fat
13.8g Total Fat
6.2g Saturated Fat
0g Trans Fat
2.1mg Cholesterol
864.5mg Sodium
27.5g Total Carbohydrates
6.6g Dietary Fiber
13.5g Sugars
13.7g Protein

Ingredients:

1 Cup of tofu, firm & diced
2 Teaspoons of cloves garlic, minced
8 Oz. of tomato paste
1 Tablespoon of garam masala

2 Tablespoons. peanut butter, creamy
10 fluid oz. of light coconut milk, canned
1 Tablespoon of curry powder
2 Cups of chunk green bell pepper
1 Cup of chunk Onion
1 ½ Teaspoons of kosher salt

Cooking Directions:

Put everything together (except the tofu) in a food processor; blend on high settings.

Place the tofu pieces in the inner part of your Instant Pot. Pour the sauce on top of the tofu pieces.

Close and lock the lid, seal the steam nozzle; set the manual option & cook for 4 minutes.

Once the cooking cycle completes, quickly release the pressure using the Quick Release option. Serve the cooked tofu pieces over some cooked rice.

Curried Potato Eggplant

Total Cooking & Preparation Time: 20 Minutes
Servings: About 2

Nutrition Facts (Estimated Amount Per Serving)
694 Calories
204 Calories from Fat
22.6g Total Fat
6.2g Saturated Fat
0g Trans Fat
50.4mg Cholesterol
2042mg Sodium
105.8g Total Carbohydrates
23.4g Dietary Fiber
27.4g Sugars
29.2g Protein

Ingredients:

1 Eggplant, medium & thinly chopped
6 Curry of chopped leaves
1 Tomato, large, crushed, chopped finely
4 Garlic cloves, minced
1 Teaspoon of coriander powder
½ Inch of ginger, minced

1 Hot green Chile, chopped finely
½ Teaspoon of each mustard seeds, cumin seeds & turmeric
1 Potato, large & cubed into small pieces
¾ Cup of water
Garam masala or pure red chili powder (cayenne) to taste
1 Teaspoon of coconut oil
Cilantro, fresh for garnish
¾ Teaspoon of salt

Cooking Directions:

Select the sauté option of your Instant and heat the oil, preferably over medium heat settings. Once the oil becomes hot; add in the mustard seeds and cumin; cook for a minute, until cumin seeds get fragrant & changes color.

Carefully add in the curry leaves and then the ginger, garlic & chili; cook until the garlic is golden, for a minute.

Add turmeric, coriander & tomatoes; mix well & cook for a minute.

Now put everything inside the bottom of your Instant Pot. Close and lock the lid to its place. Select the manual option; set the cooking for 5 minutes & cook. Once the cooking cycle completes, let the pressure release naturally. Once all the pressure is released, carefully remove the lid and give everything a good stir. Serve & enjoy!

Mushroom Matar Masala

Total Cooking & Preparation Time: 20 Minutes
Servings: About 2

Nutrition Facts (Estimated Amount Per Serving)
334 Calories
131 Calories from Fat
14.6g Total Fat
4.2g Saturated Fat
0g Trans Fat
0mg Cholesterol
809.4mg Sodium
43.7g Total Carbohydrates
12.7g Dietary Fiber
16g Sugars
15.2g Protein

Ingredients:

6 to 8 Oz white mushrooms, sliced

½ Onion, large, chopped

2 Large tomatoes,

1 Green Chile (to reduce the heat; remove the seeds)

½ - 1 Teaspoon of garam masala

5 Garlic of cloves

⅓ Cup of cashews, raw & soaked for 15 minutes

1 Inch of ginger

¾ Cup of peas or more

1 Cup of spinach, fresh & chopped (optional)

½ Teaspoon of paprika

1 Teaspoon of kasuri methi, dried (fenugreek leaves)

¼ Teaspoon of sugar or to taste

Cayenne to taste

½ Teaspoon of salt to taste

Cilantro, fresh for garnish

1 Teaspoon of coconut oil

Cooking Directions:

Puree garlic together with onion, Chile & ginger with a few Tablespoons of water in a blender, preferably on high speed.

Click the sauté option of your Instant Pot and heat the oil, preferably over medium heat settings. Once the oil is hot; added in the pureed mixture & cook until the onion smell is not raw, for couple of minutes; stirring occasionally.

In the meantime, blend cashews and tomatoes until smooth (blend in a couple of cycles), preferably in the same blender. Add this puree together with garam masala, fenugreek, and paprika to the Instant pot. Cook for 5 to 7 minutes; stirring occasionally.

Add peas, mushrooms, any other veggies, sugar, salt & ½ cup or more water; mix well.

Cover & cook until the mushrooms are cooked to your likings, for 8 to 10 minutes.

If using, this is the time to fold in the spinach, taste & adjust heat and salt to your likings. Garnish with fresh cilantro & serve over cooked grains, rice or with flat bread.

Masala Eggplant

Total Cooking & Preparation Time: 30 Minutes
Servings: About 3

Nutrition Facts (Estimated Amount Per Serving)
783 Calories
194 Calories from Fat
21.6g Total Fat
12.4g Saturated Fat
0g Trans Fat
0mg Cholesterol
738.9mg Sodium
144.7g Total Carbohydrates
35.9g Dietary Fiber
58.3g Sugars
20.9g Protein

Ingredients:

2 Tablespoons nuts, chopped such as cashews or peanuts
½ Teaspoon of mustard seeds
2 - 3 Tablespoons of chickpea flour or besan
1 Tablespoon of coriander seeds
½ Teaspoon of cumin seeds

75

2 Garlic of chopped cloves
2 Tablespoons of coconut shreds
1 - 1 ½" chopped ginger
½ Teaspoon of ground cardamom
1 Hot green chopped chile
½ Teaspoon of turmeric
A pinch of cinnamon
⅓ - ½ Teaspoon of cayenne
½ Teaspoon of raw sugar
1 Teaspoon of lemon or lime juice
½ - ¾ Teaspoon of salt
Water as needed
For Curry:
4 to 6 baby eggplants
1 Cup of water
Fresh cilantro, garam masala & coconut for garnish

Cooking Directions:

Click the sauté option of your instant pot over & sauté the mustard seeds, coriander and cumin until the coriander seeds change its color, for a couple of minutes.

Add in the chickpea flour; mix well & cook for one minute. Add in the coconut and nuts; mix well. Roast until fragrant, for a minute or two; let the mixture to cool for a minute and then transfer everything to a small food processor or small blender; blend/process to coarsely grind.

Add in the garlic, ginger, chile, lemon/lime & the remaining ground spices; pulse until you get a coarse mixture; adding a Teaspoons of water

Make cross cuts on the eggplant & fill the cross cuts with the stuffing.

Now, place the eggplants in your instant pot. Add a cup of water & ¼ Teaspoons of salt; add in a cup of cooked beans or chickpeas & cook for 3 to 5 minutes, preferably at high pressure. Once you are done with the cooking; wait for 10 minutes and let the pressure release naturally. Garnish with fresh cilantro, coconut & garam masala; serve with roti/rice or flatbread.

Mix Vegetable Masala

Total Cooking & Preparation Time: 30 Minutes
Servings: About 4

Nutrition Facts (Estimated Amount Per Serving)
278 Calories
30 Calories from Fat
3.3g Total Fat
0.5g Saturated Fat
0g Trans Fat
0mg Cholesterol
546.3mg Sodium
56.2g Total Carbohydrates
17g Dietary Fiber
14.1g Sugars
12.4g Protein

Ingredients:

3 Cups of veggies, chopped such as carrots, cauliflower, peppers, green beans, potatoes, zucchini, cabbage etc
½ Teaspoon of fenugreek seeds powder

⅓ - ½ Teaspoon of cayenne
3 Garlic cloves, minced
½ Teaspoon of each coriander, cumin, mustard, turmeric
⅓ Cup of green peas, thawed if frozen
Cilantro, fresh & lemon for garnish
½ Teaspoon of black pepper
1 Teaspoon of oil
⅓ - ½ Teaspoons cinnamon
¾ Teaspoon of salt to taste

Cooking Directions:

Mix all of the spices in a large bowl; mix well & set aside.

Click the sauté option of your Instant pot and heat the oil and then sauté the garlic until golden, for a minute. Add in the spice mix & cook for half a minute.

Instant Pot: Now, add in the veggies, splash of water & salt.

Select the Manual option & cook for a minute. Once the cooking cycle completes Quick Release the pressure and fold in the peas. Carefully remove the lid, taste & adjust the amount of salt.

Close & lock the lid again & let sit for 3 to 5 minutes. Cook on sauté option for a couple of minutes, if the veggies are not cooked. Garnish with fresh cilantro & lemon. Serve & enjoy!

Spicy Mix Veggies

Total Cooking & Preparation Time: 35 Minutes
Servings: About 2

Nutrition Facts (Estimated Amount Per Serving)
106 Calories
3.3g Total Fat
0.4g Saturated Fat
0g Trans Fat
0 mg Cholesterol
622 mg Sodium
691 mg Potassium
17.3 g Total Carb
5.3 g Dietary Fiber
4.7 g Sugars
4.6 g Protein

Ingredients:

2 Cups of cauliflower florets
¼ Teaspoon of turmeric or more
1 ½ Teaspoons of ground mustard
¼ Cup of water or more
1 Cup of sweet potato or squash or pumpkin, chopped
½ - 1 Cup of green beans, chopped

2 Greens chopped chills
½ Cup of green peas
1 Teaspoon of Panch Phoron
⅛ Teaspoon of asafetida
1 Teaspoon of oil
¼ - ½ Teaspoon of sugar to taste
1 Cup of chopped potato
½ Teaspoon of salt to taste

Cooking Directions:

Add ground mustard together with turmeric, water, cauliflower florets, potato, green beans, pumpkin & ¼ Teaspoons salt into the bottom of your Instant Pot & cook on manual settings for 4 to 5 minutes.

For the time-being, make the tempering. Over medium heat settings in a small skillet; heat the oil. Once hot, add in the Panch phoron spices & cook for two minutes, until the spices begin to pop. If the spices pop out in excess, feel free to use a lid.

Add green chilies & asafetida; cook until the chilies turn golden, for a minute.

Quick release the pressure and then add in the tempering, peas & ¼ Teaspoons salt; sauté for a couple of minutes. Taste & adjust the amount of salt & heat.

Delicious Potatoes & Peas

Total Cooking & Preparation Time: 45 Minutes
Servings: About 4

Nutrition Facts (Estimated Amount Per Serving)
209 Calories
29 Calories from Fat
3.2g Total Fat
2g Saturated Fat
0g Trans Fat
0mg Cholesterol
468.1mg Sodium
40.6g Total Carbohydrates
6.7g Dietary Fiber
6g Sugars
6.8g Protein

Ingredients:

1 Large tomato
½ Teaspoon of cumin seeds
1 Red onion, small, chopped
½ Teaspoon of red chili powder / cayenne or to taste
1 Teaspoon of mustard seeds

7 Garlic cloves
1 Inch of chopped ginger
½ Teaspoon of garam masala or to taste
1 Teaspoon of ground coriander
½ Teaspoon of ground cumin
3 potatoes, medium, chopped into ½" pieces
½ Teaspoon of turmeric
1 + cups water
¼ Cup cilantro, fresh, chopped
1 cup peas, fresh
2 Teaspoons of coconut oil
¾ Teaspoon of salt or to taste

Cooking Directions:

Click the sauté option of your Instant pot and heat the coconut oil. When hot, add in the mustard seeds & cumin; cook until the cumin seeds change its color.

Add in the onions; mix well & cook for a couple of minutes, until translucent.

In the meantime, blend the tomato, ginger & garlic until you get a coarse puree.

Add in the tomato puree & spices to the Instant pot. Cook for a couple of more minutes, until the garlic smells roasted & puree thickens.

Add in the potatoes, water & salt; cook on manual setting for 3 to 4 minutes. Once the cooking cycle completes, carefully release the pressure using the Quick Release option. Add in the spinach & peas; mix well & put the lid again on the Instant pot; let sit for a couple of minutes or sauté for a minute or two. Garnish with fresh cilantro & serve.

Vegan Butter Chickpeas

Total Cooking & Preparation Time: 25 Minutes
Servings: About 6

Nutrition Facts (Estimated Amount Per Serving)
200 Calories
95 Calories from Fat
10.6g Total Fat
7.5g Saturated Fat
0g Trans Fat
0mg Cholesterol
759.1mg Sodium
22.1g Total Carbohydrates
4.5g Dietary Fiber
3.2g Sugars
6.8g Protein

Ingredients:

1 Cup of coconut milk
1 Can of garbanzo beans, drained
1 1/4- 1 1/2 Cups of vegetable broth or water or both
1 Packet of extra firm tofu (approximately 12 Oz)
1 Teaspoons of chili powder

1/2 Cup of crushed tomatoes
1 Tablespoon of garam masala
1 Tablespoon of Curry powder
1 Cup of rice
Pepper & salt to taste

Cooking Directions:

Press any water from the tofu & cube. Add tofu together with the crushed tomatoes, garbanzo beans, coconut milk & spices to the bottom of your Instant Pot.

Close and lock the lid to its place; set the manual option and set the cooking time to 2 minutes. Once the cooking cycle completes; quick release the pressure. Carefully open the lid and add the veggie broth and rice to the Instant Pot & choose the manual settings again and set the cooking time to 4 minutes.

Once the cooking cycle completes, wait for 10 minutes and let the pressure release naturally. Serve hot with some cooked rice.

Basmati Rice

Total Cooking & Preparation Time: 20 Minutes
Servings: About 6

Nutrition Facts (Estimated Amount Per Serving)
114 Calories
23 Calories from Fat
2.5g Total Fat
0.4g Saturated Fat
0g Trans Fat
0mg Cholesterol
404.6mg Sodium
20.2g Total Carbohydrates
1.5g Dietary Fiber
2.2g Sugars
2.5g Protein

Ingredients:

1 of the medium color bell pepper
2 Cups of long-grain or basmati rice
1 Grated carrot
Water as needed

1 Medium chopped onion
1 Tablespoon olive oil
½ Cup of fresh or frozen peas
1 Teaspoon salt

Cooking Directions:

Press the sauté option of your Instant pot & swirl in the olive oil; sauté the onion until translucent, for a minute or two. Meanwhile, put bell pepper together with grated carrots in a 1L liquid measuring cup; lightly pat down into an even layer.

Transfer the water with the veggies into the container of the measuring cup until you reach 750ml mark; set aside. Add rice, peas & salt to the Instant pot; mix well & put the ingredients in the measuring cup into the Instant Pot; give everything a good stir until evenly mixed.

Close & lock the lid to its place & set the valve to pressure cooking. Select the manual option & set the cooking time to 3 minutes, preferably at high pressure. When the cooking time completes, wait for 10 minutes and let the pressure release naturally.

Once all of the pressure is released, carefully open the lid. Using a large fork; fluff the rice well & serve!

Millet & Lentils with Vegetables & Mushrooms

Total Cooking & Preparation Time: 45 Minutes
Servings: About 4

Nutrition Facts (Estimated Amount Per Serving)
146 Calories
9 Calories from Fat
1g Total Fat
0.2g Saturated Fat
0g Trans Fat
0mg Cholesterol
1035.3mg Sodium
28g Total Carbohydrates
5.8g Dietary Fiber
6.2g Sugars
7.9g Protein

Ingredients:

½ Cup of Bok Choy, sliced thinly
1 Cup of onion or leek, sliced

2¼ Cups of vegetable stock
1 Cup of millet, rinsed
2 garlic cloves, minced
1 cup sugar snap peas or snow, sliced
½ Cup of French green lentils, rinsed & picked over
Drizzle of lemon juice, fresh
¼ Cup of herbs, fresh, chopped such as parsley mixed with
garlic chives & chives
1 Cup asparagus, cut into 1" pieces
¼ - ½ Cup of oyster mushrooms or shiitake, sliced thinly
Sesame salt, for garnish

Cooking Directions:

Press the sauté option of your Instant pot; once hot, then add in the leek, garlic, and mushrooms; dry sauté for a minute or two.

Add in the lentils & millet; toast for a minute and then add in the vegetable stock. Close & lock the lid to its place; select the manual option and set the cooking time to 10 minutes, preferably at high pressure.

Once you are done with the cooking process, wait for 10 minutes and let the pressure release naturally. Once all of the pressure is released, carefully remove the lid. Add in the Bok Choy, asparagus, and peas. Place the lid again and let sit for a couple of minutes (the millet should be bright yellow).

Give everything a good stir, add in the fresh herbs & transfer everything to a large bowl. Add in the lemon juice & sprinkle sesame salt before serving.

Sweet Potato, Lentil & Coconut Curry

Total Cooking & Preparation Time: 45 Minutes
Servings: About 4

Nutrition Facts (Estimated Amount Per Serving)
234 Calories
107 Calories from Fat
11.8g Total Fat
9.7g Saturated Fat
0g Trans Fat
0mg Cholesterol
1015mg Sodium
27.2g Total Carbohydrates
7.1g Dietary Fiber
7.1g Sugars
7.2g Protein

Ingredients:

1 Carrot, large, sliced lengthwise & chopped
3 1/2 Cups of vegetable broth or water
1 Cup of red or green lentils, dried

1/2 Teaspoons of ground turmeric
1 Tablespoon of mild curry powder
1/2 Cup of coconut milk
1 Cup of diced onion
1 1/2 Tablespoon of coconut oil
Freshly ground black pepper
1 Sweet potato, medium, cut into 1" cubes
1 Teaspoon of ginger powder
1/2 Teaspoons of sea salt

Cooking Directions:

Press the sauté option of your Instant pot and then heat the oil. Sauté the onion for a minute or two, until turns slightly golden. Add in the carrot, potato, lentils & seasonings to taste; stir several times until evenly combined.

Add in the broth or water. Close and lock the lid of your Instant pot and select the manual option & cook for 10 minutes, preferably on high pressure. Once you are done with the cooking process wait for 10 minutes and let the pressure release naturally and then release any remaining pressure using the Quick Release option. Carefully remove the lid and stir in the coconut milk.

Season with pepper and salt to taste, and serve warm.

Rice & Red Beans

Total Cooking & Preparation Time: 55 Minutes
Servings: About 10

Nutrition Facts (Estimated Amount Per Serving)
Calories 274
Calories from Fat 7
Total Fat 0.7g
Saturated Fat 0.2g
Trans Fat 0g
Cholesterol 0mg
Sodium 264.7mg
Total Carbohydrates 57.5g
Dietary Fiber 4.1g
Sugars 1.3g
Protein 8.6g

Ingredients:

10 Cups of cooked rice
1 Onion, medium, diced
3 Garlic cloves, minced
1 Bell of pepper, diced
3 Stalks of celery, diced

1 Pound of red kidney beans, dry
1/2 Teaspoon of black pepper
7 Cups of water
1/4 Teaspoon of white pepper
2 Leaves of bay
1 Teaspoon of hot sauce
½ Teaspoon of thyme, dried or 1 Teaspoons fresh
1 Teaspoon of salt or to taste

Cooking Directions:

Put everything together (except the cooked rice) to the bottom of your Instant Pot.

Close and lock the lid to its place; choose the manual settings and cook for 25 minutes, preferably on high pressure.

Once you are done with the cooking, release the pressure using the quick release option. Carefully remove the lid and give everything a good stir.

Serve the cooked mixture over a cup of cooked rice.

Creamy Kidney Beans & Lentils

Total Cooking & Preparation Time: 55 Minutes
Servings: About 6

Nutrition Facts (Estimated Amount Per Serving)
250 Calories
13 Calories from Fat
1.4g Total Fat
0.3g Saturated Fat
0g Trans Fat
0mg Cholesterol
422.5mg Sodium
45.2g Total Carbohydrates
10.3g Dietary Fiber
1.4g Sugars
16.5g Protein

Ingredients:

3 Cups of Kidney Beans, cooked
1 Teaspoon of ground cardamom
6 Garlic cloves, minced
1 Teaspoon of ground turmeric

¼ Teaspoon of ground nutmeg
3 Teaspoons of ground cumin
1½ Teaspoons of chili powder, or more to taste
2 Tablespoons of grated ginger
1 Cup of whole black lentils, dry
5 Cups of water
¼ Teaspoon of ground mustard
Before serving:
2 Teaspoons of ginger, grated
½ Cup of cashew creamer
Cilantro, fresh, chopped for garnish
2 Teaspoons of tomato paste
1 Teaspoon of garam masala
Salt to taste

Cooking Directions:

Put everything together to the bottom of your Instant pot. Select the slow cooker setting & cook on low for 8 to 9 hours or for 4 hours on high heat settings.

Once you are done with the cooking; stir in all of the before serving ingredients.

Give everything a good stir & serve over brown basmati rice, preferably steamed.

Sweet Potato, Red Lentil, Hemp Burgers

Total Cooking & Preparation Time: 40 Minutes
Servings: About 8

Nutrition Facts (Estimated Amount Per Serving)
263 Calories
1.3g Total Fat
0.2g Saturated Fat
0g Trans Fat
0mg Cholesterol
14mg Sodium
1189mg Potassium
53.6g Total Carb
13.4g Dietary Fiber
1.9g Sugars
9.8g Protein

Ingredients:

1 Cup of onion, minced
2¼ Cups of vegetable stock
1 Cup of crimini mushrooms, minced

2 Teaspoons of ginger, fresh, grated
1½ Sweet potatoes, peeled & cut into large pieces
1 Cup of red lentils, rinsed & picked over
¼ Cup of hemp seeds
Vegetable cooking spray
1 - 4 Tablespoons of brown rice flour
¼ Cup of flat leaf parsley, fresh, chopped finely
1 Tablespoon of curry powder
¼ Cup of cilantro, chopped finely
1 Cup of "baby" or quick oats

Cooking Directions:

Select the sauté option of your Instant Pot electric pressure cooker. Add in the ginger, onion & mushrooms; dry sauté for a couple of minutes. Add in the sweet potatoes, lentils & vegetable stock.

Close and lock the lid to its place and select the cooking time to 6 minutes, preferably on high pressure. Once the cooking cycle completes, let the pressure come down naturally. Once all of the pressure is released, carefully remove the lid & transfer the lentil mixture to a bowl, preferably large size & let stand for 12 to 15 minutes, until cool enough to handle, preferably at room temperature.

Heat your oven to 375 F/185 C. Line a large baking sheet with the parchment paper & lightly coat it with the cooking spray.

Mash the lentil mixture with a fork or a potato masher, when cool. Stir in the cilantro, parsley, hemp seeds & curry powder; and then stir in the oats. Now is the time to add the brown rice flour using the tablespoon, if the mixture seems to be too wet.

Form the mixture into 8 to 10 patties using wet hands and place each patty onto the already prepared baking sheet. Bake for 8 to 10 minutes; flip & bake until they are firm & brown, for 10 more minutes.

Let cool for couple of minutes. Serve immediately, freeze, or refrigerate for later use.

Cranberry Sauce

Total Cooking & Preparation Time: 25 Minutes
Servings: About 3

Nutrition Facts (Estimated Amount Per Serving)
200 Calories
7 Calories from Fat
0.8g Total Fat
0g Saturated Fat
0g Trans Fat
0mg Cholesterol
6.8mg Sodium
52.6g Total Carbohydrates
2.8g Dietary Fiber
46.5g Sugars
0.1g Protein

Ingredients:

¾ Cup of cranberry juice cocktail
1 Cup of cranberries, dried
¾ Cup of water
1 Teaspoon of lemon juice, freshly squeezed

Cooking Directions:

Put everything together to the bottom of your Instant Pot. Close & lock the lid to its place. Select the manual option and set the cooking time to 3 minutes, preferably at high pressure.

When the cooking time completes, wait for 10 minutes and let the pressure release naturally. Once all of the pressure is released, carefully remove the lid and give the mixture a few quick pulses to partially puree the contents using an immersion blender; to speed up the thickening process, just break some large parts.

Let the mixture simmer for 3 to 5 minutes, until you get your desired thickness, stirring frequently & preferably un-covered. Turn off the heat, once you can see the bottom & drag a spatula or spoon across the base of the cooker. Let stand for 8 to 10 minutes, preferably un-covered.

Serve warm & enjoy or tightly cover & refrigerate for up to a week.

Apple Crisp

Total Preparation & Cooking Time: 20 Minutes
Total Servings: 3

Nutritional Value (Estimated Amount Per Serving)
436 Calories
147 Calories from Fat
16.3g Total Fat
9.8g Saturated Fat
0.0g Trans Fat
41mg Cholesterol
506mg Sodium
451mg Potassium
77.0g Total Carbohydrates
10.2g Dietary Fiber
54.5g Sugars
2.3g Protein

Ingredients:

5 Apples, medium, peeled, chopped into small chunks
3/4 Cup of rolled oats, old fashioned
1/2 Teaspoon of nutmeg

1 Tablespoon of maple syrup
1/4 Cup of brown sugar
4 Tablespoons of vegan butter
1/4 Cup of flour
1/2 Cup of water
2 Teaspoons cinnamon
1/2 Teaspoons salt

Cooking Directions:

1. Fill the bottom of your Instant Pot with the apple chunks. Sprinkle the chunks with nutmeg & cinnamon. Top with maple syrup & water.

2. Melt the butter completely. Mix melted butter together with the flour, oats, salt & brown sugar in a small bowl. Drop the batter on top of the apples using spoonful.

3. Close and lock the lid of your instant pot. Select the manual option & set the cooking time to 8 minutes, preferably on high pressure.

4. Once the cooking cycle completes, release the pressure using the natural release option. Let sit a couple of minutes until the sauce thickens.

5. Serve warm or topped with vanilla ice cream.

Thank you

for buying our book!

I hope Air Fryer Cookbook is helpful for you!

I am constantly looking for way to improve my content to give readers the best value so If you didn't like the book I would like to also hear from you! Please feel free to give your honest opinions as this could help me make improvements.

Finally, if you enjoyed this book, would you be kind enough to leave a review for this book on Amazon?

Thank you and good luck!

54779609R00060

Made in the USA
Middletown, DE
06 December 2017